I Am Here For You!

A Story to Support Your Grieving Child Through Death From Substance Use

Pronoun of Person Who Died: He/Him

Puddle Jumper Publishing

Copyright © 2022 Puddle Jumper Publishing
Published by Puddle Jumper Publishing
www.puddlejumperpublishing.com

All rights reserved. No part of this publication may be reproduced, stored in a retrieval system, or transmitted in any way or by any means, electronic, mechanical, photocopied, recorded or otherwise, without the prior written permission of Puddle Jumper Publishing. For information regarding permission, write to Puddle Jumper Publishing, puddlejumperpublishing@gmail.com.

Book design by Sarah E. Holroyd (https://sleepingcatbooks.com)

Paperback ISBN: 978-1-7777138-6-7
Ebook ISBN: 978-1-7777138-0-5

Author and Illustrator
Carla Mitchell, M.S.W., R.S.W

Tips for Reading This Story with a Child

Read the story to become comfortable with the content before reading it with your child. Throughout the story are helpful talking tips to keep the conversation going.

This book is designed to explain death in concrete terms. It is important that your child understands what death means and has the language to talk about it.

Instead of saying "Your Person" try saying the name of the person who died.

At the end of each page, pause for a breath, provide comfort and the opportunity for questions. Some children may be naturally curious about death and have many questions.

Honesty is the best approach. Even if the information is difficult, it is best if your child hears it from a trusted adult first. This teaches your child that they will be included when difficult things happen in the family and that it is okay to talk about them.

Follow your child's lead and answer their questions as factually as possible. You do not have to provide more details than asked for.

It is okay to say that you don't know the answer, or encourage your child to share their own thoughts by asking "What do you think?" or "I wonder about that too."

Avoid euphemisms. Words such as "passed away," "gone," "lost" or "sleeping" can be confusing for children. Use the words dying, dead and death.

Nature provides many opportunities to talk about death with children. This image of a tree was selected to help you draw connections to nature. The tree was near a chemical spill. The substance went into the tree and poisoned it. Perhaps it was a sudden accident (substance poisoning) or a slow leak that eventually poisoned the tree (substance use disorder).

Learn more about how children grieve by exploring websites dedicated to children's grief. See the resource list at the back of this book.

This book belongs to:

_____

In memory of:

_____

You can still love Your Person
Even when you're apart.
The memories you have
Keep him in your heart.

Talking Tip: As an adult, it is beneficial to show and name your own emotions. Reassure the child that they did not cause you to feel sad by saying "I feel sad because he died. It is okay to feel sad when someone dies." Modelling feelings of grief to children can help them understand, name and express their own emotions.

A sad thing has happened,
Come sit by my side.
When you want to talk about
Your Person who died.

You won't make me upset,
I like to talk about him too.
Even if I get tears
In my eyes when we do.

It is okay to talk
About how **Your Person** died.
Talking can help us
Feel better inside.

I Am Here For You!

Talking Tip: Help the child to understand that death is a natural and normal event that happens to all living things. Take opportunities to talk about death as you see them in the real world (example: a dead flower or a squished bug). If your child asks if you (or they) will die be honest, "Yes, someday I will die, but I hope that it won't be for a long time because my body is healthy."

A tree starts as a seed,
That grows up to the sky.
One day it falls down,
Because all living things die.

Trees die in nature,
For many different reasons.
Like diseases, accidents or
Growing old with the seasons.

This tree was near an accident
Where a chemical spilled
A substance went into the roots
And the tree was killed.

I Am Here For You!

Talking Tip: Help the child understand the life cycle. As trees and humans age, there are signs that the body is changing. How old was the person who died? Was he a seed (pregnancy/birth), a sapling (baby/child), a young tree (teenager), a mature tree (adult) or an aged tree (old age)? Ask the child what they know and understand about death.

All living things will die,
Yes, this is true.
It happens to plants, animals,
Pets and people too.

People usually die
When they grow to old age.
But death can happen
At any time or stage.

Death means that the body
Has stopped working inside.
It happens to all living things,
Like Your Person who died.

I Am Here For You!

Talking Tip: This tree died because a substance/chemical entered into its roots and poisoned it. This may have been a sudden accident (substance poisoning/overdose) or a slow leak (substance use disorder/addiction). People may use substances for many reasons: recreational, to feel different, prescribed, peer pressure, unknowingly… A substance use disorder happens when a person cannot stop using substances even if they want to.

Your Person died from a substance
That made his body very ill.
A substance is a chemical
Like a drug, alcohol or pill.

Substances make people act
Unlike they normally do.
They may hurt themselves or others
Even when they don't mean to.

A substance caused his body
To stop working inside.
A poisoning or an overdose
Is how Your Person died.

I Am Here For You!

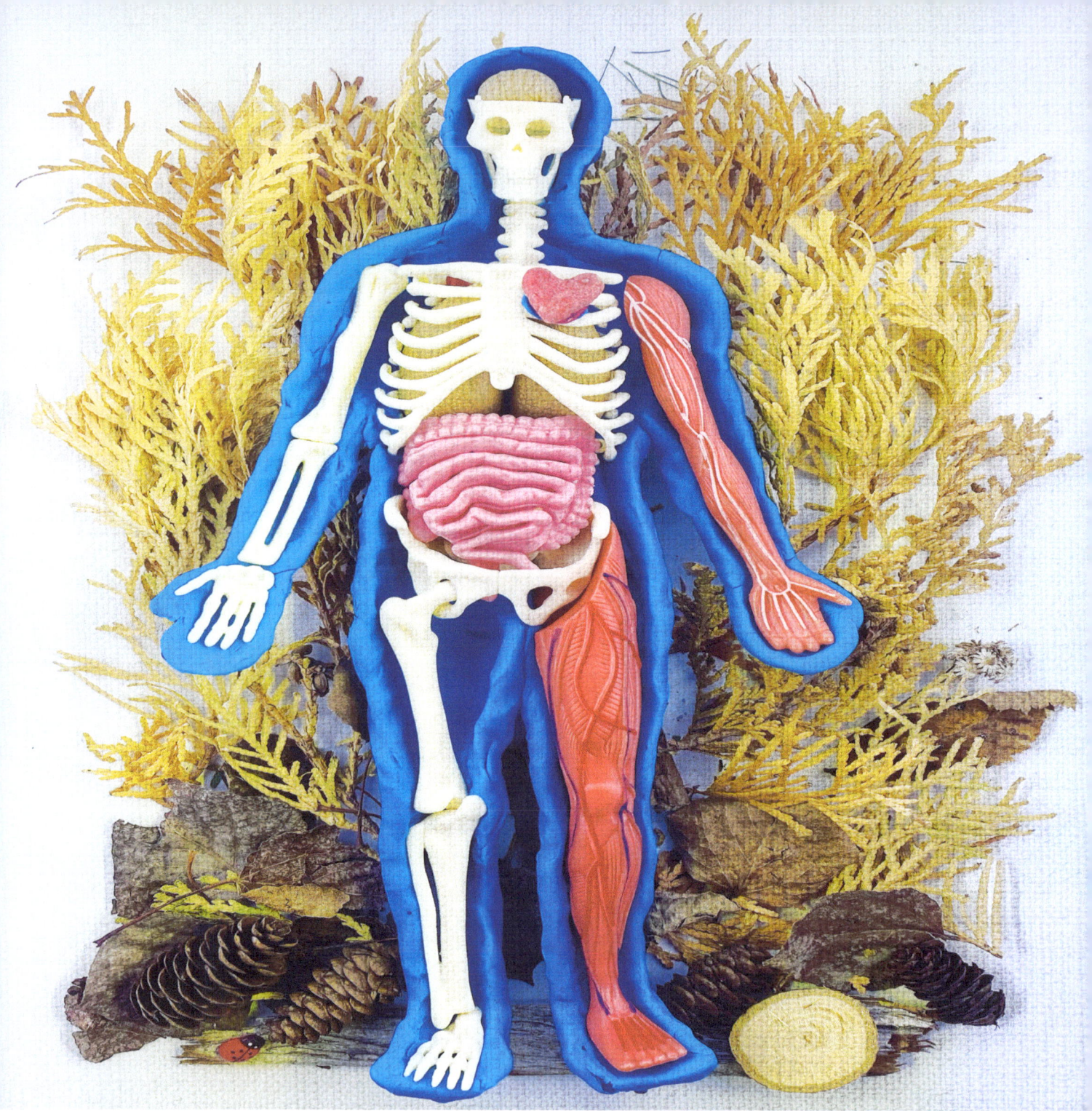

Talking Tip: Help the child to understand that death means the body has stopped working. For example: "The substance caused his heart to stop beating. The heart pumps blood around the body. When the heart stops working the body dies." Children need help to understand that death is permanent and once the body stops working it cannot become alive again.

From the bottom of the feet,
To the top of the head,
The body doesn't move
When it is dead.

The heart doesn't beat,
The lungs don't breathe air,
The body doesn't talk or eat,
Walk, feel or grow hair.

Your Person's body stopped working,
It won't come back to life one day.
When the body is dead
It stays that way.

I Am Here For You!

Talking Tip: Reassure the child that they did not cause the death to happen and that it is not their fault. Funerals are a way to say goodbye to the body, by burial or cremation (using a white-hot heat to turn the body to ash that looks like sand). Attending a funeral is helpful for children who want to participate, but they should not be forced to attend.

I want you to know,
You are such a good kid.
This didn't happen because of
Anything you said, thought or did.

Death is hard to understand,
We don't always know why.
We wish we could change it
And not say goodbye.

Your Person's death
Was not your fault, you see?
We could not have stopped it,
Not you or not me.

I Am Here For You!

Talking Tip: Reassure the child that their feelings are normal and help them name their emotions. Listen and validate their grief, "I see your tears, it is okay to be sad that Your Person died." Children express their emotions in many ways, such as: verbally, repeatedly asking questions, playing games with death themes, creating art, having behavioural regressions, sleep disturbances, changes at school and more.

When Your Person died,
It changed many things.
Grief is the mixed-up thoughts
And feelings death brings.

Grief can make you cry tears,
When you feel upset or sad.
Grief can make you shout,
When you feel angry or mad.

Grief can be confusing,
Your shoulders might shrug.
Grief can be scary,
And you might want a hug.

I Am Here For You!

Talking Tip: Children's grief has been described as puddle jumping – one minute they are deep in the grief and the next minute they go back to playing. Even if they don't appear to be, children are still grieving. Children may grieve with each new stage of development as they better understand death and the impact that it has on their lives. Like adults, grief is a life long process that changes over time.

Grief can make you feel guilty,
Like you've done something wrong.
Grief can come and go
And the feelings can last long.

How grief feels can change,
Depending on the day;
We can still be happy,
Smile, laugh and play.

Did you know that adults
Have grief feelings, too?
I miss Your Person,
Just like you do!

I Am Here For You!

Talking Tip: Reassure the child that they will be cared for and loved. Children may feel isolated or misunderstood following the death of someone important to them. Reassure the child that they are not alone. It can be helpful to identify a number of people who will be there for them including: other family members, understanding friends, teachers, peer support groups and counsellors (if applicable).

I will love you no matter
How your grief feels each day.
I am always here to listen
And help you on the way.

Things will get better,
Together we will cope.
We have each other,
To heal and share hope.

You are not alone,
So many people care.
Your friends, family and teachers
Will also be there.

I Am Here For You!

Talking Tip: Children benefit from having opportunities to remember their person, speak about them and share memories. Children often worry that talking about their person will make the adults around them sad, so it can be helpful for adults to bring up the person who died. Facilitate memory sharing by using the tips at the back of this book.

One thing I know,
Is that Your Person loved you.
We will never forget
How special he is to you.

We will remember Your Person
By speaking his name,
And doing the things he loved,
Like a special meal or game.

We will stay connected,
Through stories, pictures and art
Because remembering him
Keeps him in your heart.

I Am Here For You!

My Grief Story

My Grief Story

My name is _____.

I was ____ years old when my _____ died.

His name was _____.

He died from _____.

He died on _____.

My grief sometimes feels like
_____ or _____.
I know all the feelings I have are allowed and okay.

People who will help and care for me are
_____ or _____.

Things I wonder about...
_____?

Things to Remember

Things I Always Want to Remember

Foods he liked: _____

Activities he liked: _____

Music he liked: _____

Games he liked to play: _____

His favourite thing to do: _____

My favourite thing about him: _____

My favourite memory: _____

My least favourite memory: _____

Something he always said: _____

Something else: _____

Ask other people to share photos or write down their favourite memories of Your Person to keep inside of a memory box.

Ways of Remembering

Ways of Remembering

Share stories and memories

Light an electronic candle

Keep photos around the house

Draw a picture or create art

Make a memory box

Keep a comfort item (example: shirt)

Visit the grave or memorial site

Create an online memorial

Make Your Person's favorite meal

Practice cultural or spiritual traditions

Start a new tradition in his honour

Remember birthdays or anniversaries

Write a letter to the person who died

Plant a tree in his memory

Feeling the Feelings

Feeling the Feelings

Take some deep breaths

Let your tears out

Punch something soft and safe – like a pillow

Spend some time in nature

Attend a peer support group

Write in a journal

Draw a picture

Spend some quiet time remembering Your Person

Do some exercise or go for a walk

Talk to an adult or friend you trust

Talk to a teacher or counsellor

Practice a guided meditation

Attend a children's grief camp

Listen to music that reminds you of Your Person

Favorite Pictures or Keepsakes

Favorite Pictures, Drawings or Keepsakes

Suggestions for these pages:
Glue/tape favorite pictures, store keepsakes such as a funeral card, draw a picture of the person of died, draw a picture of a favorite memory, write down special stories of the person or write a letter to the person who died.

Favorite Pictures, Drawings or Keepsakes

Favorite Pictures, Drawings or Keepsakes

How My Heart Feels Activity

Instructions: Your child can choose colours to represent different grief emotions (example: blue = sad or red = angry). Then fill in the heart using colours that represent how they feel. You can do this activity with your child by drawing a heart on a piece of paper. Talking about emotions together helps model healthy grieving.

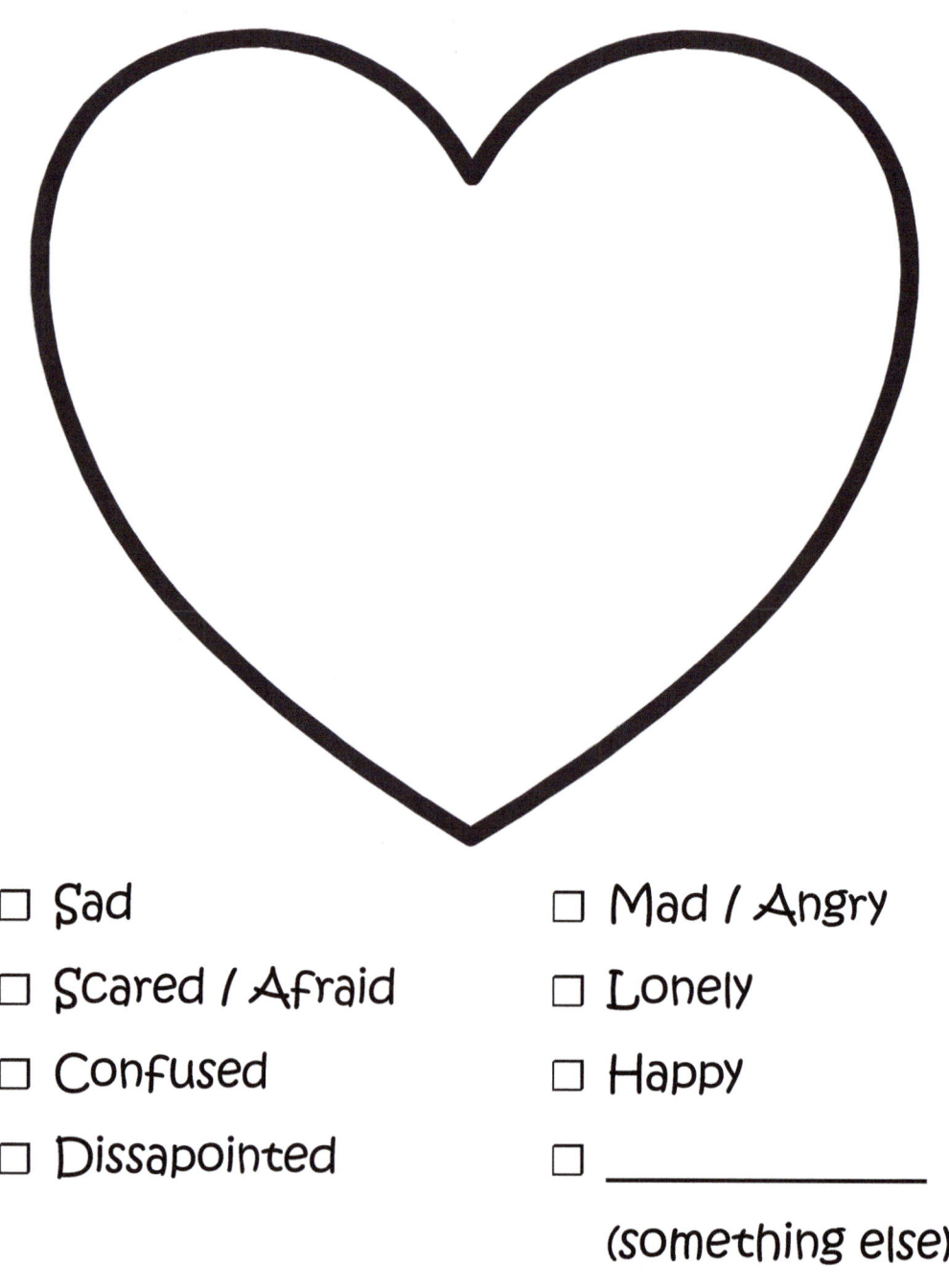

- ☐ Sad
- ☐ Scared / Afraid
- ☐ Confused
- ☐ Dissapointed

- ☐ Mad / Angry
- ☐ Lonely
- ☐ Happy
- ☐ _____

(something else)

Grief Emotions

For instructions to make your own Hope Stone visit:
www.puddlejumperpublishing.com

A Guide to Explaining Death from Substance Use

Tell the Truth: young children benefit from being told the truth about what happened. Honest and clear information from a caring adult helps them begin to process grief and adapt to their changed reality.

Use Simple Words and Descriptions: young children need simple explanations and definitions to help them understand what death is and how their person died.

> Death/Dead: "means the body stopped working inside"
>
> Substance use death (accidental overdose or poisoning): "your person used more of the substance than their body could handle and it caused their body to stop working inside".
>
> Addiction: "is an invisible disease in the body that causes a person to want more and more of a substance (alcohol, medicine or drugs) than is safe". An addiction is a disease. Some children worry they will develop an addition too; provide reassurance that there are ways they can prevent addiction.

Stigma: death from substance use can be stigmatized in society. Help the child understand that substance use doesn't mean their person was a bad person. Reassure the child that their person did not use substances because of something they did and that the death was not their fault.

Listen: allow the child to share as much of their story as they want to. Be open to listening without judgement or trying to minimize/distract them from their feelings. Children need to be free to express their emotions, even the really big and difficult ones.

Grief Reactions: children may experience a wide range of emotions, including sadness, guilt, regret, confusion, fear, anger, shame and more. Children may feel conflicted about their relationship with the person who died.

Encourage: encourage the child to think, talk about and practice ways of expressing their emotions. Being able to "get out" their upset feelings and thoughts helps (examples: write in a journal, talk to a caring adult or express though art, music or physical activity).

Ongoing Support: grief is a life long journey and children will require ongoing support.

Resource List

There are many excellent resources available to help you support your grieving child at home and in school. Visit our website to find additional resources specific to death from substance use. If you are concerned about your child, seek professional help.

Puddle Jumper Publishing
www.puddlejumperpublishing.com
Follow on Facebook, Instagram and TikTok

Canadian Virtual Hospice
www.kidsgrief.ca (learn about children's grief)
www.youthgrief.ca (a site for grieving youth)
www.mygrief.ca (learn about adults' grief)

Children and Youth Grief Network
www.childrenandyouthgriefnetwork.com

Canadian Alliance for Children's Grief
https://grievingchildrencanada.org/

Children's Grief Foundation of Canada
https://childrensgrieffoundation.org/

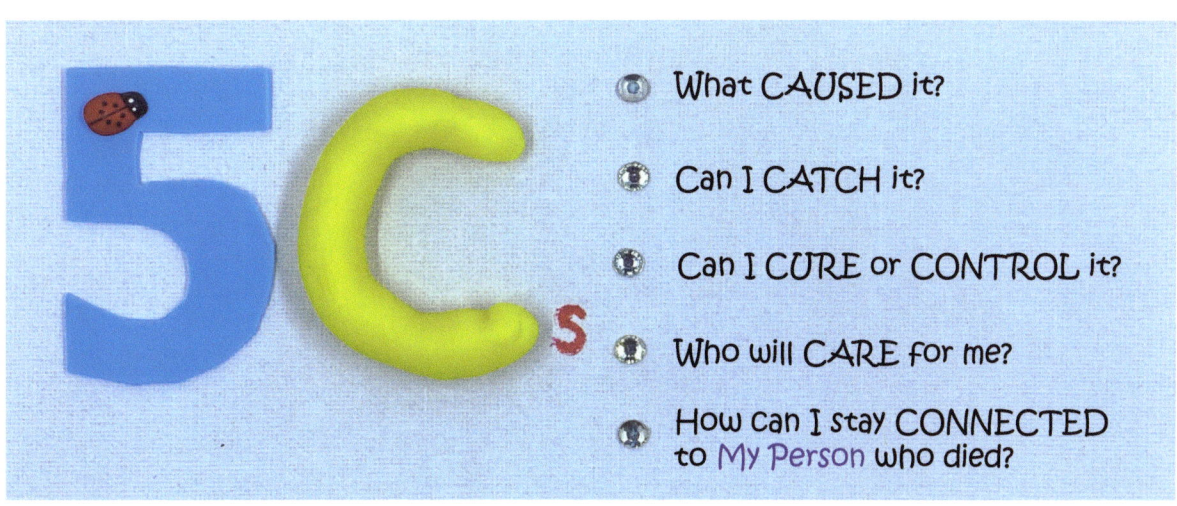

About the Author

Carla Mitchell holds a Master of Social Work degree from the University of Regina and is a trained End of Life Doula. She specializes in grief and bereavement support for children, families, adults and organizations.

She is also the mother of three young children who are grieving. Her books were inspired by her professional practice and personal experiences of explaining death to her own children.

Grief is a life long journey and it changes over time. Children benefit when their caring adult is able to have open conversations about death and feelings of grief. These conversations can be difficult, but they are so important!

If you are caring for a grieving child, please remember to care for yourself too.

Holding space for you in grief and healing,
Carla Mitchell, MSW/RSW
Puddle Jumper Publishing

www.ingramcontent.com/pod-product-compliance
Lightning Source LLC
Chambersburg PA
CBHW042248100526
44587CB00002B/68